WHAT WE SHARE

WHAT WE SHARE

Collected Meditations, Volume Two

COLLECTED BY
PATRICIA FREVERT

SKINNER HOUSE BOOKS
BOSTON

Published by Skinner House Books. Skinner House Books is an
imprint of the Unitarian Universalist Association, a liberal religious
organization with more than 1,000 congregations in the U.S. and
Canada. 25 Beacon Street, Boston, MA 02108-2800

Printed in Canada.

Cover design: Suzanne Morgan

Text design: WordCrafters

ISBN 1-55896-423-1

Library of Congress Cataloging-in-Publication Data
What we share / collected by Patricia Frevert.
    p. cm. — (Collected meditations ; vol. 2)
  ISBN 1-55896-423-1 (alk. paper)

    1. Meditations. 2. Spiritual life—Unitarian Universalist
churches—Meditations. 3. Unitarian Universalist churches—
Prayer-books and devotions—English. I. Frevert, Patricia. II.
Collected meditations ; v. 2.

BX9855.W48 2002
242'.809132—dc21

                                                              2001048355

5 4 3 2 1
04 03 02 01

The selections included here were previously published by Skinner
House Books as follows: *In the Holy Quiet of This Hour,* Richard S.
Gilbert, 1995; *Blessing the Bread,* Lynn Ungar, 1996; *Taking Pictures of God,*
Bruce T. Marshall, 1996; *Evening Tide,* Elizabeth Tarbox, 1998.

TABLE OF CONTENTS

WHAT IS HOLY?

Meditation, or prayer, offers each of us nourishing moments of calm, the chance to look within, to reflect on our experience. Whether taken alone or in community, such moments are opportunities to be enriched and strengthened.

The meditations in this collection have been selected from meditation manuals published each year by the Unitarian Universalist Association. Unitarians and Universalists have been publishing annual editions of prayer collections and meditation manuals for more than 150 years. In 1841 the Unitarians broke with their tradition of addressing only theological topics and published *Short Prayers for the Morning and Evening of Every Day in the Week, with Occasional Prayers and Thanksgivings.* Over the years, the Unitarians published many volumes of prayers, and in 1938, *Gaining a Radiant Faith* by Henry H. Saunderson launched the tradition of an annual Lenten manual. During the late 1860s, the

Universalist Publishing House was founded to publish denominational materials. Like the Unitarians, the Universalists published Lenten manuals, and in the 1950s they complemented this series with Advent manuals. Since 1961, the year the two denominations combined to form the Unitarian Universalist Association, the Lenten manuals evolved into meditation manuals, reflecting the theological diversity of the two denominations.

Grounded in the belief that no single religion has a monopoly on wisdom or inspiration, the four writers of these meditations draw on many faith traditions—Christianity, Judaism, Buddhism, and other of the world's great faiths.

PATRICIA FREVERT

AN AFFIRMATION

In the love of beauty
and the spirit of truth
we unite
for the celebration of life
and the service of humanity.

RICHARD S. GILBERT

WHAT WE SHARE

WHAT WE SHARE

Let us celebrate the common rituals that make us kin:

The poignancy of welcome and farewell,
The anguish of defeat,
The tender touch of those who call us friend;

The exuberant joy of birth,
The empty space in our hearts when a loved one
    dies,
The ultimate loneliness that each knows,
The warm embrace of comrades who welcome us to
    the celebration of life;

The questions that persist and perplex and do not
    yield to our need for answers,
The shining moments when the sun slants across
    our dim meandering path and illuminates the
    way,
The strange and anxious excitement of moving on
    to new places to call home;

The fragments of frustration when our best efforts
    yield pitiful results,
The helplessness we feel in a world that sometimes
    presents only problems,
The high joy when some small victory for humanity
    is won and we have helped it happen;

In all our moments of doubt and despair, of prob-
    lem and pain,
Let us remember the common lot shared by our
    human kin.

In all our times of truth and triumph, of faith and
    fortitude,
Let us celebrate what we share.
We are, after all, in this together.

RICHARD S. GILBERT

INCARNATION

The trees have finally
shaken off their cloak
of leaves, redrawn
themselves more sternly
against the sky. I confess
I have coveted this
casting off of flesh,
have wished myself
all line and form, all God.

I confess that I am caught
by the story of Christmas,
by the pronouncement of the Spirit
upon Mary's plain flesh.
What right did the angel

have to come to her
with the news of that
unprovided, unimaginable
birth? What right
had God to take on flesh
so out of season?

When Mary lay gasping
in water and blood
that was of her body
but not her own
did she choose one gleaming,
antiseptic star to carry
her through the night?

The flesh has so few choices,
the angels, perhaps, none.
The trees will shake themselves
and wait for spring.
The angels, unbodied, will clutch
the night with their singing.
And Mary, like so many,
troubled and available,
will hear the word:

The power of the Most High
will overshadow you

and in her flesh, respond.

LYNN UNGAR

AUTUMN EQUINOX

You may think of it
as marking the long descent,
the slide into winter's weariness.
Such moments are not easy to accept—
don't we all want to petition
some cosmic governor
to grant summer a reprieve?
But the sentence is always cast,
the scales will always tip,
whatever you might think is just.

In this brief, breath-catching
moment at the top
you may recall the slow climb of summer,
the safe, steady ticking up the tracks.
The self-possessed might even
gaze out and glimpse
the jostling fairgrounds and
the quiet that stretches beyond the fence.

Look quickly. Even now the car
tips forward and picks up speed.
As the wind in your face increases
and your stomach leaps, remember:
This is the ride you came for,
the fear and the sense of flying.
Winter won't seem long

when you slide to a halt
around the final curve.

LYNN UNGAR

THE EMPTY CHAIR

There is something about an empty chair
That reminds us of our ultimate loneliness,
Evoking memories of those we have loved and lost.
No longer will they occupy that chair,
However much their image is etched in our memory.

Chairs know the comings and goings of people,
The assault of young bodies
And the gentler weight of old ones.
They know the passing of the years;
They absorb all in well-worn wood.

There is something in us
That doesn't like an empty chair,
That wants it occupied
By the ones we love and loved.
Its presence haunts us with memories that fade
But do not die.

We reach out across empty space,
Encircling nothing but a memory.
Our fingers caress the well-known cracks and grooves,

As familiar to us as the body that filled them.
Our eyes create the image of a former time
When loved ones brought a chair to life
And endeared it to us.

Now there is little to do but sit,
Supported by the strength of years,
Occupying beloved space for a time,

Rejoicing in times gone by, never to return.
People, like chairs, are full of memories,
Memories that sustain our coming in and our going
    out
From this day forward.

RICHARD S. GILBERT

VALENTINE

Creation gives us snow.

Lest we imagine beauty was only for summer, or trees for leafing; just in case we thought cold was for winter or, at best, firesides or pots of pea soup, creation gives us snow.

Creation outlines each slender twig with snow, a flake at a time. With divine patience, winter writes a character, a syllable, a word, until nature's grace is there on every tenacious surface.

And what of you and me? Ought we to think we can do better in our building of trust that we dare hurry such a thing as friendship?

Let us write our vows slowly, knowing some of the words like snowflakes will fall away, that from time to time a misunderstanding will come like a gust of wind or a bird's foot to a snow-covered branch, disrupting the careful gifts of love. Let us work on our manuscript, mirroring nature's patience, until the love is whole and the drift of our days is done.

ELIZABETH TARBOX

THANKSGIVING

I have been trying to read
the script cut in these hills—
a language carved in the shimmer of stubble
and the solid lines of soil, spoken
in the thud of apples falling
and the rasp of corn stalks finally bare.

The pheasants shout it with a rusty creak
as they gather in the fallen grain,
the blackbirds sing it
over their shoulders in parting,
and gold leaf illuminates the manuscript
where it is written in the trees.

Transcribed onto my human tongue
I believe it might sound like a lullaby,
or a child's prayer before bed.
Across the gathering stillness
simply this: "For all that we have received,
dear God, make us truly thankful."

LYNN UNGAR

MASKS

What will you wear for Halloween?
The trees are changing faces, and the
rough chins of chestnut burrs
grimace and break to show their
sleek brown centers. The hills
have lost their mask of green and grain,
settled into a firmer geometry
of uncolored line and curve.

Which face will you say is true—
the luminous trees or the branches underneath?
The green husks of walnuts, the shell within,
or the nut curled intimately inside,
sheltered like a brain within its casing?

Be careful with what you know,
with what you think you see.

Moment by moment faces shift,
masks lift and fall again, repainted
to a different scene. It means,
the cynics say, there is no truth,
no constant to give order to the great equation.

Meanwhile, the trees, leaf by leaf,
are telling stories inevitably true:
Green. Gold. Vermillion. Brown.
The lace of veins remaining
as each cell returns to soil.

LYNN UNGAR

BLESSING THE BREAD

Baruch atah Adonai, Eloheinu melech ha'olam, hamotzi
lechem min ha'aretz.

Surely the earth
is heavy with this rhythm,
the stretch and pull of bread,
the folding in and folding in
across the palms, as if
the lines of my hands could chart
a map across the dough,
mold flour and water into
the crosshatchings of my life.

I do not believe in palmistry,
but I study my hands for promises
when no one is around.
I do not believe in magic.
But I probe the dough
for signs of life, willing
it to rise, to take shape,
to feed me. I do not believe
in palmistry, in magic, but
something happens in kneading
dough or massaging flesh;
an imprint of the hand remains
on the bodies we have touched.

This is the lifeline—
the etched path from hand
to grain to earth, the transmutation
of the elements through touch
marking the miracles
on which we unwillingly depend.

Praised be thou, eternal God,
who brings forth bread from the earth.

LYNN UNGAR

LONELINESS AND LOVE

Loneliness is our common fate.
There is no escape.
But out of that loneliness comes our salvation,
For we love out of our fear of being alone.
As long as human beings people the earth,
We can be assured
That in our loneliness
There is also love—
Deep, infinite love,
Waiting to be tapped,
To water the barren brown lawn of our loneliness—
Love which shrivels if kept to the self,
Which flourishes only if it is given away.

I need you.
You need me.
I know it.
You know it.
What are we waiting for?

RICHARD S. GILBERT

LENT

The season of Lent takes place on the Christian calendar for forty days before Easter.

Lent does not exactly catch the popular fancy. Many of the references I hear trivialize it: "This year I'm giving up liver for Lent." Or treat it as an opportunity for commercial promotion: "Macaroni and cheese! The perfect meal for Lent!"

Lent is defined as a time of fasting and penitence in preparation for Easter. In this day and age both fasting and penitence may seem peculiar.

And yet during this season of Lent—when the earth is still barren from winter—our lives too may seem on hold, waiting for a miracle.

It's a time when I become deeply aware of the sufferings in the congregation, the community, the world. On any given day we all look pretty much all right, but beneath the appearances many struggle.

It's a time when I revisit the sorrows I have caused others. Old memories that hide from summer's sun and spring's brilliant colors and the excitement of fall activities—these make themselves known during this fallow time of the year.

It's a time when "doing without" seems the appropriate way to nourish our spirituality. As the earth still is "doing without," as we reach the end of our store of energy and spirit that was gathered and packed away during the harvest. Now we do without and await a word of hope—the promise of a future.

Religious liberals sometimes are accused of wanting Easter without Lent or Good Friday. Given our attitude of hope and affirmation, we may skip past the struggles that give birth to new life.

But I have not found that to be true. Suffering and struggle come to us, whether there's room in our theology for it or not. The faith that speaks to this experience is not specifically Christian but universal—that there is meaning in our struggles, that we may be transformed in our suffering, that Easter awaits beyond the barrenness of this season of Lent.

BRUCE T. MARSHALL

HEALING

I observed the period between Christmas and New Year's Day in the traditional manner—I got sick. I don't know what I had. It may have been some hybrid of cold and flu. All I know is that I was sick.

When you're sick the world feels different. Everyday pleasures cannot be depended on—the smell of coffee, the taste of breakfast, the gift of sleep—none of these is available. Everyday challenges become just about insurmountable.

Healthy people don't know what it's like to be sick. Even healthy people who were sick the week before—they forget. They bustle around making unthinking assumptions that we who are sick do not share.

One of those assumptions is that we are in control of our lives. When we're sick we're not in control—we can't will ourselves back to health. I sat around drinking plenty of fluids and taking aspirin and gobbling Vitamin C tablets and trying to stay warm. But none of that was going to cure what I had.

At best such activities prepare the way, make conditions right for the cure to take place. But the cure itself is something that happens, not something I do.

This probably is true for more things than we would like to admit. We prepare conditions for what we hope may occur—healing, renewal, transformation. But then we wait for something else to take over. Something else that actually does the healing, renewing, transforming.

It takes getting sick to remind me of that. I may think I have my destiny in my own hands, but really what I'm doing is becoming open and available for whatever it is that truly does the healing, renewing, transforming.

BRUCE T. MARSHALL

HOW DOES SANTA DO IT?

I came across a study conducted by psychologists from Harvard and Yale that may shed light on the age-old question: How does Santa Claus do it? How does he keep fit year after year despite a breakneck schedule?

In this study, two groups of nursing home residents (Santa, after all, is no youngster) of similar age, socioeconomic status, and emotional and physical health were selected. Each person was given a plant.

Members of one group were told that the plant was theirs to take care of and that its fate would depend on their efforts. They also were told that they were competent men and women who should be making decisions for themselves.

People in the other group were told that their plants would be looked after by the nursing home staff just as the staff took care of them because, after all, they were in the home to be cared for.

Within a few weeks the researchers found a noticeable difference between the two groups. Those who cared for their own plant showed an increase in emotional and physical well-being and a visible increase in activity levels. Eighteen months later, the mortality rate of this group was only half that of the other.

A theme of the holiday season is giving. Giving, of course, can become obligation and a cause of considerable stress, but it also enhances our lives as it connects us with others. We are reminded of those who are important to us and who depend on us. Our gifts are in thanks for those who keep us involved in life.

Santa Claus, after all, is overweight, smokes a pipe, and lives on a diet of cookies and milk (whole milk, not skim). How does he do it?

It's probably all that giving and caring—and those people depending on him—that keeps him such a healthy and happy old elf.

BRUCE T. MARSHALL

THE POIGNANCY OF LIVING
IN THESE DAYS

THE POIGNANCY OF LIVING
IN THESE DAYS

I inhale and exhale in regular rhythm,
An act so common it never occurs to me to pay
    attention.
And when I do, I am overwhelmed with the wonder
    of it all.

I eat my food, as I have done for a thousand thou-
    sand days,
A practice so frequent I hardly notice
The miraculous million events that happen in my
    body.
And when I do, I am taken with their singular
    beauty.

I greet my loved ones, as I have greeted them for
    years,
A habit that I pass off casually
Until I realize the deep poignancy of greetings and
    farewells,
How precious they are,
How they touch deeper feeling chords each time.
Perhaps it is middle age, or old age,
Or perhaps sentiment grows in me,
Or perhaps I am awakening to life
In ways transcending my usual semi-awake state of
    being.

The poignancy of living in these days
Penetrates me, burrows deep into psyche or soul or
    spirit—
I know not what.
I only know that I feel things more deeply with the
    passing years,
That the common things of life become uncommon,
That the ordinary becomes extraordinary,
That the habitual becomes sacred.
Bittersweet is the poignancy of living in these days.
I awaken myself,
And bow down in deep gratitude.

RICHARD S. GILBERT

GROUNDHOG DAY

Celebrate this unlikely oracle,
this ball of fat and fur,
whom we so mysteriously endow
with the power to predict spring.
Let's hear it for the improbable heroes who,
frightened at their own shadows,
nonetheless unwittingly work miracles.
Why shouldn't we believe
this peculiar rodent holds power
over sun and seasons in his stubby paw?
Who says that God is all grandeur and glory?

Unnoticed in the earth, worms
are busily, brainlessly, tilling the soil.
Field mice, all unthinking, have scattered
seeds that will take root and grow.
Grape hyacinths, against all reason,
have been holding up green shoots
beneath the snow.
How do you think that spring arrives?
There is nothing quieter, nothing
more secret, miraculous, mundane.
Do you want to play your part
in bringing it to birth? Nothing simpler.
Find a spot not too far from the ground
and wait.

LYNN UNGAR

THE LONG WALK HOME

Out walking one morning I saw a medium-sized
turtle begin the dangerous journey across the road
from one side of Monponsett Pond to the other.
The traffic is pretty heavy, even at 6 a.m., and as the
turtle left the safety of the roadside grasses, I looked
right and could see a line of cars coming, led by a
Harley-Davidson ridden by a leather-clad figure in a
tinted Plexiglas helmet. The turtle was almost at the

halfway point, destined for extinction beneath those burning wheels. I moved a few paces into the road and simply pointed to the turtle. The motorcyclist slowed, bringing his gleaming bike to a stop. He put out his arm to indicate to the cars behind him that they should not overtake. He allowed the turtle to cross in safety. Then he and I signaled a greeting to each other and went on our ways.

The turtle, the motorcyclist, and I were on different journeys that day, and mine was a journey of discovery. I discovered that compassion sometimes wears a motorcycle helmet. I found the place inside me that fears bikers and I made a few corrections. I don't know what kind of day the turtle had, or the person on the motorcycle, but my day was better for having encountered them.

ELIZABETH TARBOX

HOPE, NOT OPTIMISM

A friend whose wife is undergoing treatment for a serious illness told me that their physician advised them to approach it with hope, not optimism. My friend found this guidance helpful, and it makes sense to me.

Optimism, as I understand it, is an attitude of expectation that a particular result will occur—that a person will recover from an illness, that we will achieve a specific goal, that the Publishers Clearing House will pick my number from among the billions submitted. The dictionary defines optimism as "an inclination to anticipate the best possible outcome."

Hope is less specific. It's an attitude that looks for possibility in whatever life deals us. Hope does not anticipate a particular outcome, but keeps before us the possibility that something useful will come from this.

We are told that an optimistic outlook is a good thing, but I've rarely found it so. Optimism often leads to disappointment. When the best possible outcome doesn't occur, we are let down, may even feel betrayed. Optimism then may become its opposite—pessimism, an inclination to anticipate the worst possible outcome.

Hope is more resilient, more enduring, more helpful. In a serious illness, for example, there are often setbacks. In the face of these, optimism may wear down. But hope encourages us to move forward despite the setbacks.

As we pursue our goals in life, optimism may lead us to expectations that are unrealistic and ultimately hurtful. Hope advises us to look squarely at the realities that confront us while remaining aware of the possibilities.

Erich Fromm observed, "To hope means to be ready at every moment for that which is not yet born, and yet not become desperate if there is no birth in our lifetime. Those whose hope is weak settle for comfort or for violence; those whose hope is strong see and cherish signs of new life and are ready every moment to help the birth of that which is ready to be born."

It is helpful guidance, I think, whether we are faced with a serious illness, a personal dilemma, or a society that seems determined to destroy itself—not optimism that a particular result will occur, but hope to "see and cherish signs of new life" wherever these may occur.

BRUCE T. MARSHALL

THANKS BE FOR THESE

For the sound of bow on string,
Of breath over reed,
Of touch on keyboard;

For slants of sunlight through windows,
For shimmering shadows on snow,
For the whisper of wind on my face;

For the smooth skin of an apple,
For the caress of a collar on my neck;

For the prickling of my skin when I am deeply
   moved,
For the pounding of my heart when I run,
For the peace of soul at day's end;

For familiar voices in family rites,
For the faces of friends in laughter and tears,
For the tender human arms that hold me;

For the flashes of memories that linger,
For the mysterious moments that beckon,
For the particularity of this instant;

For the silence of moon-lit nights,
For the sound of rain on my roof,
Of wind in dry leaves,
Of waves caressing the shore;

For the softness of summer breezes,
For the crispness of autumn air,
For dark shadows on white snow,
For the resurrection of spring,
For the faithful turning of the seasons;

For angular, leafless trees,
For gentle hills rolling in the distance,
For meandering streams seeking an unseen sea;

For cornstalks at stiff attention,
And brittle plants bristling past their prime,
For unharvested gardens returning plants to enrich
    the soil;

For the sight of familiar faces,
The sound of our spoken names,
The welcoming embrace of outstretched arms;
For the ritual of friendship,
Reminding us we matter:
Thanks be for these.

RICHARD S. GILBERT

CRAB GRASS

We've all admired it
even as we've cursed
the matted roots, white fingers
pointing toward new frontiers,
the tangled tapestry stubbornly
weaving the world in place.

Imagine living that way.
Imagine knowing from the ground up
that you are tied to the whole,
that you are undefeatable,
that below the surface

undefinable discoveries
are always taking place.

Don't you think there are
things worth holding on to
with a thousand arms,
ten thousand gripping toes?
Aren't the undaunted
particularly blessed?

Before you deride the faithful
consider carefully
where you will put your roots.

LYNN UNGAR

MEDITATION FOR MOTHER'S DAY

I stood out at the low-tide mark early in the morning, and looked back at the shore a quarter of a mile
away. Trees whose every branch I know when I am
standing beneath them blended with their neighbors, and I could not recognize them. I found
myself looking at small segments of the shore and
wondering: if a sliver was all I could see, would I
know it to be my beach in the morning light? Or
would I know it only if I could see it all, in one
majestic arc of familiar landscape? Do I know it well
enough so when I cannot see it, it is still there in my

memory, fresh and sweet? Is it always available in the parts of my being that cannot be left behind?

Do I know you well enough, so that I would recognize you from a great distance, from the tilt of your head, the sway of your step, or the merest whisper of your voice? Have I looked carefully at you, and noted the texture of your skin and the color of your eyes, so that when you are miles from here, I can see you easily in the space reserved for the most precious memories?

Have I trusted you enough, so you know who you are, and can be sure of yourself in a world that doesn't want to trust? Have I modeled the life I want you to live, one of caring and appreciation and feelings and love? And have I learned all I can from you, so I can draw on your wisdom and lean on your truth, even when we are far apart?

And have I loved you enough, so that you will know you are loved when the storms beat you down, the friendships disappoint, or the demands of a world that needs your love weigh too heavily on your shoulders?

Have I said thank you to the creative spirit who brought our lives close enough to touch, and who gave us the chance to notice one another and dwell together in this moment?

Then let me give thanks now.

ELIZABETH TARBOX

HARD LOOKS

I was in my backyard when I heard someone shout from beyond the hedge, "I could *do* it if you wouldn't look so hard."

This was a child's voice. I had no idea what she was trying to do, but I knew exactly what she was saying. Everything is more difficult when people "look so hard."

When I was a teenager, my neighbor had a basketball hoop mounted on his garage. I spent hours practicing lay-ups, jump shots, and free throws. I invented methods of getting the ball through the hoop that didn't yet have a name. In the process I developed a certain grace in handling ball and basket.

Then gym class came, and we were instructed in the basketball fundamentals. We each had to show our skills in front of classmates—teenaged boys: certainly among the hardest lookers in the business. My agility disappeared. I had no access to the skills developed at my neighbor's basketball hoop. I became my old clumsy self.

As we grow older, we internalize hard looks. There doesn't have to be anyone around, and we still feel eyes trained on us. It happens to me sometimes when speaking at a service, when in conversation, when going about an ordinary task: I feel the hard looks. Then I stiffen, grace leaves me, I'm back in eighth-grade gym. (On a recent occasion I was trying to be so relaxed I turned around and walked straight into a table.)

When I was a child, there were neighbors who lived about four houses away: two elderly women and a man. On summer evenings they would sit on their porch and I would ride my bicycle up their sidewalk to visit. I don't remember what we talked about. What I remember is that they listened to me and were interested in what I told them, and they liked me. I was afraid of some old people because they seemed critical, but these neighbors were comfortable and never gave hard looks. With them I could be myself.

Our own children will grow up feeling the glare of hard looks. I don't know any escape from that. But perhaps they also will experience times and places and communities of softer looks. Then as they grow into adulthood, their views of themselves may not be so harsh. They will know the grace of self-acceptance, the release of self-forgetfulness.

When not followed by hard looks, there are wondrous things we can do.

BRUCE T. MARSHALL

FOR THOSE WHO HAVE REARED US

(Inspired by "The Invocation to Kali" by May Sarton)

We give thanks for those who have reared us,
Who have nourished us through sleepless nights and
 restless days,
Who have seen us through the good times and the
 bad,
Who have celebrated our triumphs
And suffered through our defeats.
We are grateful for their nurturing spirit,
Their gentle touch and their firm hand,
Their familiar laugh and their sympathetic tears.

We acknowledge the unpleasant times as well,
Our struggle to separate ourselves
As children who must make their own way in the
 world.
We realize our times of ingratitude and selfishness
And resolve to make amends.

We pay silent tribute to the loved ones no longer
 among us,
And speak soft thanksgiving to those who are.
May we who have been nurtured
Also be nurturers of those who follow;
May we be part of that current of humanity
That courses through time and space.

May we be "gardeners of the spirit"
Even as we have been tended by loving hearts and
    hands.
On this day may we commingle gratitude
For those who nourished us
And commitment for those
Who receive the gift of life and love from us.
May we be worthy.

RICHARD S. GILBERT

BATS

Perhaps you have not loved
this miracle—the bats
on their flickering wings
ushering in the night.
Certainly these days the darkness
comes too soon, and dimness
has outlasted color. But still,
there is the way they love
what you do not desire,
the way they appear, like stars,
without arriving. There is the
way their furred bodies shimmer
above the earth like angels,

the way they hear what we
have lost. Haven't you always
longed for wings? Imagine
hanging by your toes in some
cave or tree or belfry,
how gently the darkness opens,
how the night is filled
with imperceptible singing.

LYNN UNGAR

BAY ROAD

The tide is high now. Through the wintering sticks
of next year's hedge, I can see the marsh move
above the restless motion that circles the earth and
disturbs the sunlight. Outside my sliding glass door a
tree full of brown sparrows earns the appellation
"thickly settled." The sparrows and pink-fronted
finches scrabble for their places on the three feeders, until a jay comes along and unbalances them all.
So close, only a glass wall to keep them from coming
in the house, or me from reaching into their tree.
But our friendship is based on respect, and they are
as little likely to enter my space, as I theirs.

I shall leave this place soon and do not know when I shall again live as aqueous a life. I have woken to the laughing call of seabirds and slept to the gentle reassurance of the siren on the Gurnet Lighthouse nearby. I have stroked lightly through the ripple of moonbeams across the bay at midnight and fingered the old weathered wood of the rickety dock. I am filled with this beauty, and I have to trust that the filling will last. For the world is a broken place, and I need to remember the irresistible force of water and the way it moves forward to cover the cracks just a little at a time, and the easygoing flexibility of the little dock that weathers all storms. And it is a brave world, too, full of adventure for those who do not hold on tight to the moorings, or close their eyes to the beckon of morning.

I promise not to forget. I promise that in mornings to come, though I stare from another window, I shall remember the view from this one. In warm summer afternoons, I shall picture the water lapping against the steps and the movement of mini ice floes in the winter. I shall feed other birds and hear other comforting sounds, but I shall not forget this place and the love it has shown to my soul.

ELIZABETH TARBOX

A TOMB IS NO PLACE TO STAY

A tomb is no place to stay,
Be it a cave in the Judaean hills
Or the dark cavern of the spirit.

A tomb is no place to stay
When fresh grass rolls away the stone of winter cold
And valiant flowers burst their way to warmth and
    light.

A tomb is no place to stay
When each morning announces our reprieve,
And we know we are granted yet another day of
    living.

A tomb is no place to stay
When life laughs a welcome
To hearts that have been away too long.

RICHARD S. GILBERT

A COMPLICATED CHRISTMAS

I wish for you this year a complicated Christmas. Not
the Christmases of simple joys and warm memories
that we feel obligated to strive for, but a season in
which there is room for the complexities that occur
during this time.

A season of complicated memories, of happiness and pain, of comfort and loss, of disappointment and fulfillment.

A season of gifts, some that remind us of the relationships that sustain us, some that remind us of the silliness and excess to which we are also subject.

A season of joy that also has room for sadness, because gladness and sorrow take place together. A season of busyness that also grants us time to pause. A season of bustling that also allows time for quiet. A season of celebrations that also encourages time for reflection.

A season of stories and songs about which we have complicated feelings. Some fill us with the warmth of nostalgia, some make us cringe with discomfort, and some bring messages of truth and hope that we still yearn to hear.

A season of light that brings us to see more intensely the shadows of our lives. A season of hope that underscores how far we still must travel to realize these dreams.

It is in this world of complicated feelings and memories that a star appears and shines above, drawing us forward with promises of peace and goodwill, offering glimpses of the path that still lies ahead.

BRUCE T. MARSHALL

HOMECOMING

I returned at sunrise to my special beach at Shipyard Lane, where morning is a soft line on the horizon and the trees have been touched by the fastidious brush of spring. And I walked slowly to the edge of the sweet ocean that moves and calls me, and I dipped my fingers in her hair and tasted the salt and knew I was home.

I want to bring you the warm smell of spring there; re-create for you the twist of a certain old wild apple tree with branches frosted with blossom, or hum the song of the chorale that sounds from every branch. I want you to place your bare feet down on that cool sand, and draw your breath deep into your own secret inner world where your truth and only your truth is spoken.

I want to press your hands lightly to the smooth grey rocks and show you the chipmunks that make their home between the rocks and the beach plum bushes. But if that cannot be, if you and I are too far apart, or don't even know each other's names, then know at least that Shipyard Lane gives me more love than I can use, plenty enough to share. And I would share it with you.

ELIZABETH TARBOX

LETTING GO OVER THE FALLS

We approached the falls from upstream,
Hearing only a roar designed to intimidate the faint-
    hearted.
At first glance we saw only white water cascading
    over the cliff
And plunging into the pool in front of us.
The thought that I might be in that water tumbling
    from an unknown height
Kept my heart pounding, adding to the modest
    exertion of the hike.
At last we came into full view:
A lonely mountain river plunging fifteen feet or so,
Swirling through rapids and around rocks to other
    falls
One definitely would not want to ride.

Stripping to a bathing suit and an old pair of
    pants—
So as not to rip my one and only swimsuit
And foreshorten my North Carolina swimming
    career—
I plunged into the lovely pool beneath the falls
To make my way to the point of ascent.
One had to move into the swift current
And then drift to the cable anchored in the rocks.
Clumsily I pulled myself up the rocky slope to the
    top,

Hand over trembling hand.
Surely, there was no turning back now.
After all, had not my two sons already made the
    plunge
And lived to tell the tale exuberantly?

I sat in the edge of the stream and nothing hap-
    pened.
I did not move.
I slowly slid to the center of the stream

But the current did not take me.
I am not certain I wanted to move.
I pushed myself deeper into the stream's center.
Gradually I lost control.

Quickly the current pushed me toward the edge
And even more quickly hurled me over the falls.
I plummeted like a great stone,
Mouth open in a smile of joy or look of terror, I've
    forgotten which,
Down into the deep pool—deeper and deeper.
I could not touch bottom.
Some primordial instinct had me swimming for the
    air
And I broke the surface water to my own relief
And to the applause of an assembled group
No doubt eager to see if this particular Unitarian
    Universalist divine
Could really walk on water.

Unable (or unwilling) to perform this feat, I swam
    for the rocky shore
To repeat the process with something approaching
    confident joy.

There is something to be said for letting go,
For risking the uncertain,
For putting oneself in strong life currents
With a rich mixture of faith and fear.
Unknown pools sustain us, buoy us;
Forgotten instincts stretch our spirits to the surface
Where the air is clear and the water cold and
    refreshing.

RICHARD S. GILBERT

TIDE PULL

TIDE PULL

Where does the tide go
when it moves out?
Following the moon
in its predictable ellipses,
what hole or foreign shore
takes up the water that has left?

When the net of light has hauled
the ocean off to sea,
does the starfish wonder
at its loss, left naked as a hand
upon the rock that was the ocean floor,

or is there some crustacean
form of faith that holds
the tidepool creatures steady as
the world turns daily upsidedown?

The moon is full tonight.
What does this signify
about the tide? What does it mean
to the starfish, or to love or faith
or any of the cyclic resurrections
we unwillingly endure?

If I stand naked on
this rock, howling for
the water's safe return,

will you, who are the moon,
remember me? If in

these hours devoid of water
I opened out my hands
to catch the light, would I
be party to the moon's ascent,

or would you drop me
in the last retreating wave,
leave me afloat or foundering,
without a chart to map
what phase or tide would
draw me finally to shore?

This is the final edge.
There is no space between the
water and the sand, no rock
that gives a guarantee. Caught
within the waves' continual
cresting and retreat, there is no choice
but learn the starfish rhythm
of a shifting home.

LYNN UNGAR

NOVEMBER MORNING

There was a snow goose this morning, and a crescent moon still visible through the freshly revealed branches of the maple, so recently leafed in yellow. The goose flies with its strong neck stretched out, and its broad wings lifting it powerfully over the restless waves. The red dawn braces over the horizon, and my crows wail that winter is coming.

And the lone wild bird flies on, never knowing that across the bay lives a man with a rifle, who shoots ducks for sport and leaves them to die in the water. Or perhaps the bird knows and flies on; perhaps the bird knows what we know, that the world is a place of beauty, and of madness, of violence, and of compassion. Perhaps the spirit that moves the bird to flight also moves in us to commit love in response to anger, and kindness where there has been killing.

I believe that love will prevail and peace will rule the earth only when we can bring ourselves to be fully, openly present to the pain that violence causes, when we know in the deepest, most truthful place in ourselves that each act of hatred tears at the fine web of life to which we are all attached, and must be countered by acts of healing. When we dare to feel another's pain, we shall be so deeply affected that we will not turn aside, but rush to be healers, lovers, friends.

ELIZABETH TARBOX

WINTER INTO SPRING

The trees, along their bare limbs,
contemplate green.
A flicker, rising, flashes rust and white
before vanishing into stillness,
and raked leaves crumble imperceptibly
to dirt.

On all sides life opens and closes
around you like a mouth.
Will you pretend you are not
caught between its teeth?

The kestrel in its swift dive
and the mouse below,
the first green shoots that
will not wait for spring
are a language constantly forming.

Quiet your pride and listen.
There—beneath the rainfall
and the ravens calling you can hear it—
the great tongue constantly enunciating
something that rings through the world
as grace.

LYNN UNGAR

SEASONS

The early snow reminds me that the seasons are changing. Apple season is about over. Grapefruit season will soon begin.

Apple season starts with the first hint of autumn on a summer night. A night when you are awakened by winds that sound different from summer storms or summer breezes. These foretell a change and have a hint of coolness in them. That's when apple season begins. It doesn't end until Thanksgiving has passed, when the leaves are gone from the trees, when the calendar turns to December. Then grapefruit season begins (and orange season and cinnamon and clove season).

Ovaltine season overlaps apple and grapefruit season. It starts later than apple season—you can't have warm Ovaltine early in September but you can certainly eat an apple then. Proper Ovaltine season needs a night cold enough for the heat to go on in your house. Then, with the warm/dusty/comforting smell of the furnace's awakening, you reach for the Ovaltine.

Some speak of a summer season for cold Ovaltine. I don't think so. Not when you can cool off with a Brooklyn egg cream (recipe: chocolate syrup, seltzer, and a splash of milk). Cold Ovaltine is like the advice on the back of the oregano jar: "Use when preparing peas, eggplant, carrots, beef or lamb stew, pot roast." Nonsense. Oregano is for pizza. Period.

Asparagus season starts as early in the year as you can manage. February is best, but March will do. It's the first vegetable to reassure us that winter will end. Rhubarb is the second. Ovaltine season can overlap asparagus and rhubarb seasons, but not by much. The furnace may still be going at full blast, but now it's time to think of iced peppermint tea. (This is the same reasoning that brings us to don short-sleeved shirts on the first hint of a spring sunny day.)

Some seasons are very short. Strawberry Quik, for example. Once every five years. The season lasts about eight minutes and then is gone. The last time it came through, I must have been asleep. It's better that way.

But some seasons never end. Chocolate. Warm bread. Hot coffee. Peanut butter. They're different in each phase, but always in season, always in style. Sort of like that wine that used to be advertised as perfect for white meat and red.

Offer chocolate, warm bread, hot coffee, and peanut butter, and you'll never be embarrassed by being out of season.

BRUCE T. MARSHALL

A NEW MEXICO EDUCATION

The red rocks won't let my eyes alone. Drawn into their hard clear lines, stark against the sky, my small self is made even smaller.

Standing beneath its silence I am afraid of being crushed by this mountain. At its crest I am afraid of falling. Neither of those things is going to happen, so it is something else, this spasm in my stomach. As I stare into the rock, notice the spruce standing tall at the mesa top, roots going god-knows-how-deep into the volcanic tuff of this mountain, I am immobilized by my insignificance. That's it. I am nothing. I am nothing to this mountain, to that tree, except as I die and add my dust to the scant topsoil between the crevices.

Self-delusion is the universal human trap. We believe in our importance and reinforce that hour by hour, in our loveless use of the earth, and especially in our religion. We have raised ourselves to the potency of mountains and tell each other it is God's plan.

But the truth is, this mountain is big. It is enduring. If God has a plan, it surely includes this mountain. And we are small, and lie to one another about our size to keep from feeling afraid.

As I stare and reflect and face the truth, I am released from my need to be noticed. I can stare at this mountain and see that it is beautiful, and I can take this beauty into myself and it will fill me up.

ELIZABETH TARBOX

THE PEAR TREES

There they stand,
two ancient pear trees long past their prime.
They have survived many seasons of ice and snow,
    wind and weather,
though they show their wounds.

Their pears are hard and beyond eating.
They seem to be all bark with no center,
so hollow that one can easily see through them.
Yet life continues to surge through their veins.
Will they burst into bloom again?
Will the leaves come on strong
to hide their worn-out branches?

What keeps them going, year after changing year?
Some ancient hunger for life, no doubt,
a desire to live, to grow and produce.
I cannot yet bring myself to cut them down,
though I fear some strong wind will end them soon.
But who is to know?

And so they stand in silent witness
to the persistence of life.

RICHARD S. GILBERT

CORMORANTS

This is what passes
for silence in the city.
You have fallen asleep
beside the lake, oblivious
to the roar of traffic
behind the trees. I
am watching the cormorants
out on the buoys, drying
their feathers in the sun.

Wings outstretched, they
look like pictures I have seen
of the first Christians
in prayer, crucifixes set
in disorderly rows. It hurts
when I raise my arms
to imitate their posture.
It is an attitude of receptivity
that few of us can afford.

The cormorants, of course,
have no alternative.
Their primitive feathers
do not repel the water
like a duck's, and so they
wait here til the sun
has dried them well
enough to dive or fly.

Ancient renunciates
in their drab black, they
have no firm place
in water or in air, but only
this peculiar stance
of openness in the place between.

I confess I am perplexed,
caught somehow
between your oblivion
and the cormorants,
empty as sundials, pointing
themselves at the sky.
How can you sleep
in such a public place, amidst
the bicyclists and fishermen?
If I opened my arms,
what would let go?

"Pray always," said the saints,
wrapped like the birds
in some prehistoric grace
that I have never understood.
"Pray always." Meaning,
I suppose, your head on
my knee, the bicycles, the city
which is never silent, where we
must, nonetheless, be still.

LYNN UNGAR

NOW WINTER COMES

Now winter comes, its labored breath misting the morning, frost sparkling on the pier. Exposed now, the birds make no pretense of shyness, smothering the feeders, fueling against the cold.

In March I didn't welcome spring's celebration, exploding from every limb's end; but today I am not ready to batten down for winter. Give me another morning to stand coatless before the awakening dawn.

But pine boughs have already been wreathed and bowed, and fir trees cut and limbed for countless living rooms. So let me breathe good fresh air and wrap my coat around me.

And let our hearts warm to smells and smiles of winter. Let us hold hands against the cold and sing carols to season winter with merriment. And with hopeful hearts, let Christmas be received.

ELIZABETH TARBOX

SNOW

I love snow.

I love the beauty of snow. I like to watch it through a window as it transforms familiar landscapes. I like to walk in it at night and absorb its soft glow. Snow brings wonder and magic.

I love the quiet of snow. When I lived in Manhattan, a storm dropped over a foot of snow on the city. I woke up that morning to an unaccustomed sound—silence. The traffic had stopped and the din of commerce and shouts from the street were gone. For a few hours the city was a different place.

I love the sense of community that snow brings. We come together in uncommonly good humor during a snowstorm. I don't think we ever talk quite so easily with friends and strangers as when it snows.

I love the gift of time a good snowstorm brings. Meetings and classes are called off. We find ourselves with an unexpected day or evening to ourselves. Usually I fill my life with plans. A snowed-out night shows me that there is more to life than what I have covered.

I don't like the weather people on television who fuss and grumble at the thought of snow and who like their weather only warm and sunny. To my mind, warm and sunny is overrated. It's nice for a change, but too much of it makes us dull and complacent.

Besides, there is no thrill on a warm and sunny day of coming into a cozy house with a cup of hot chocolate, settling into a soft chair to read or dream or gaze through the windows as the world outside is transformed.

BRUCE T. MARSHALL

PLAIN FLIGHT

The air is alive with the
commonest birds: pigeons,
starlings, crashing in waves
against the ever-opening sky.
Perhaps the wind is tossing
the birds like leaves.
Perhaps the spinning flocks
make the wind.

Ignorant, earthbound, I want
to open my mouth and be filled
with flying. I want to be full
of ordinary wings, with the flow
of bodies roped together by air,
with the visible unwinding
of patterns in time.

I want my plain self magnified
by movement, expertly caught
and carried by wind. I long,
I suppose, for the glorification
of the simplest angels, to be part
of the known unfolding. To be drawn
into and drawing the design.

Open a bag and the birds will settle,
caught by crumbs or a scatter
of grain. It isn't hard to empty

the sky of magic. But tell me:
What is it that I must open
if I would empty myself
into the turning air?

LYNN UNGAR

PAS DE DEUX

My morning walk takes me alongside Monponsett
Pond. The ways of the pond are new to me, the mist
that curls over the surface and is swept up by the
first strong tongue of sunlight, the dozen shades of
grey the pond wears according to the season and
time of day.

But the greatest gifts of this pond and my morning walks are two blue herons. The herons fly over
the pond, not a foot above it, so the tips of their
wings, in performance art, kiss the sealed surface
without breaking it. Their reflections fly beneath
them, rhythm without melody, feathered beauty lifting my soul through the day.

This is a reminder: if life finds you flying without
the grace of a blue heron, let your spirit breathe each
day, find a moment in your morning for the healing
power of beauty and the expression of gratitude.

ELIZABETH TARBOX

LIFE IS ALWAYS
UNFINISHED BUSINESS

LIFE IS ALWAYS
UNFINISHED BUSINESS

In the midst of the whirling day,
In the hectic rush to be doing,
In the frantic pace of life,
Pause here for a moment.

Catch your breath;
Relax your body;
Loosen your grip on life.

Consider that our lives are always unfinished
    business;
Imagine that the picture of our being is never
    complete;
Allow your life to be a work in progress.

Do not hurry to mold the masterpiece;
Do not rush to finish the picture;
Do not be impatient to complete the drawing.
From beckoning birth to dawning death we are in
    process,
And always there is more to be done.

Do not let the incompleteness weigh on your spirit;
Do not despair that imperfection marks your every
    day;
Do not fear that we are still in the making.

Let us instead be grateful that the world is still to be
    created;
Let us give thanks that we can be more than we are;
Let us celebrate the power of the incomplete;
For life is always unfinished business.

RICHARD S. GILBERT

ELLIS ISLAND

You reach the Ellis Island Museum by the same boat
that stops at the Statue of Liberty. The museum is
housed in the main building that received over 12
million immigrants. Forty percent of America's pop-
ulation can trace its roots to relatives who entered
through Ellis Island.

When I walked into the building I felt the presence of these people, their first steps onto American
soil, the place where they were to be received and
evaluated. I sensed their hope, their fear, and sometimes their desperation. The new immigrants often
showed no emotion until they were granted official
entry. Then: rejoicing.

The pictures the museum has gathered tell such
stories. There are faces that were hopeful, exhaust-
ed, puzzled, stern. There was elation from those who
were accepted and dejection from those turned

away. An unforgettable photograph shows a group of men with chalk marks on their coats, indicating that they were to be returned.

One section of the museum is dedicated to the diversity of the American people and the many places we come from. Some of us came to America with a dream and some of us came as slaves. All struggled to make it in this new land. Some enjoyed successes, others found a hard life awaiting them. But through it all is a vision: people coming from different places and nationalities and races and religions to make one nation. My response was unexpectedly emotional. (I wasn't the only one blinking tears.) I felt patriotic in a way that flags and military bands never touch.

My grandparents arrived at Ellis Island from Germany before World War I. After they were established in America, they sent for my grandfather's father. When he reached Ellis Island there was a hitch. He waited but was not received by immigration officials. For three days he sat in the cavernous waiting room.

My grandparents knew what boat was bringing him to New York and that it had arrived. When they didn't hear from him, they made frantic inquiries. He was sought out at Ellis Island and found, waiting. For three days his name—Dege—had been called over the loudspeaker but mispronounced.

When my great-grandfather finally was granted
entry into this country, my grandparents received a
telegram, *"Ich bin frei!"*

BRUCE T. MARSHALL

OVERWHELMED BY BEING

There are times when we feel overwhelmed by
 being,
We are on a treadmill walking hurriedly, going
 nowhere;
The images of our lives fly past us as on a movie
 screen,
The hands of the clock we see actually moving—too
 quickly.

At such times we need to gather ourselves together,
Slacken our pace,
Blank out the screen,
Ignore the clock.

Then we can remind ourselves that we are in charge
 of our lives,
That it is we who dictate the pace,
We who can choose to stop the rapidly moving
 screen,
That we can set the rhythm of our own lives.

It will not be easy—it is never easy to convert
    ourselves,
To turn ourselves around,
To get some kind of handle on the story of our own
    lives,
To realize that we are the architects of our own fate.

To be sure, there are powers and principalities that
    confront us;
The demands on our time and energy are endless,
We cannot fully control our environment;
We are, after all, finite and flawed creatures.

But out of that finitude comes a yearning for
    meaning,
Out of the flawed nature of our being we yearn for
    purpose,
Out of the hectic rush of events we can still set our
    own pace.
We are the only ones who can.

RICHARD S. GILBERT

BREAKING GROUND

Living in the violence of Spring
Living in a time
where shells are cracking

and shapes alter
Who can afford to risk
forgetting the danger
forgetting the moment
the crocus bulb breaks ground
Never knowing whether
snow or sun or ice
awaits in warm or jagged welcome

There is no safety in
this restless season
Even the sheltering ground
rejects its own,
thrusting the life it held
into the untrustworthy
and insufficient care
of air and weather

There are no choices here
No careful path or
reasoned way
No holding in reserve for
some more settled,
more propitious time

But only the unconsidered
faith of the crocus
whose saffron petals echo
or demand the sun

LYNN UNGAR

THE COURAGE OF PATIENCE

When we are overwhelmed with the world
And cannot see our way clear,
When life seems a struggle between tedium and
    apathy
Or frenzy and exhaustion,
When today seems a punishment and tomorrow a
    torment,
May we find the courage of patience.

May we recognize courage in ourselves and our
    companions
That is not dramatic, that elicits no fanfare,
That commands little notice by the world,
That is forgotten and taken for granted.

May we learn how to cope
Like those who live one day of pain at a time,
Who see the long path of suffering and do not
    despair,
Who inspire us by their patient courage,
When we are impatient and afraid.

May we know such courage
And quietly celebrate its presence among us.

RICHARD S. GILBERT

CAMAS LILIES

Consider the lilies of the field,
the blue banks of camas opening
into acres of sky along the road.
Would the longing to lie down
and be washed by that beauty
abate if you knew their usefulness,
how the natives ground their bulbs
for flour, how the settlers' hogs
uprooted them, grunting in gleeful
oblivion as the flowers fell?

And you—what of your rushed
and useful life? Imagine setting it all down—
papers, plans, appointments, everything—
leaving only a note: "Gone
to the fields to be lovely. Be back
when I'm through with blooming."

Even now, unneeded and uneaten,
the camas lilies gaze out above the grass
from their tender blue eyes.
Even in sleep your life will shine.
Make no mistake. Of course
your work will always matter.
Yet Solomon in all his glory
was not arrayed like one of these.

LYNN UNGAR

PASSOVER

Then you shall take some of the blood, and put it on the door posts and the lintels of the houses. . . and when I see the blood, I shall pass over you, and no plague shall fall upon you to destroy you, when I smite the land of Egypt.

—Exodus 12:7&13

They thought they were safe
that spring night, when they daubed
the doorways with sacrificial blood.
To be sure, the angel of death
passed them over, but for what?
Forty years in the desert
without a home, without a bed,
following new laws to an unknown land.
Easier to have died in Egypt
or stayed there a slave, pretending
there was safety in the old familiar.

But the promise, from those first
naked days outside the garden,
is that there is no safety,
only the terrible blessing
of the journey. You were born
through a doorway marked in blood.
We are, all of us, passed over,
brushed in the night by terrible wings.

Ask that fierce presence,
whose imagination you hold.
God did not promise that we shall live,
but that we might, at last, glimpse the stars,
brilliant in the desert sky.

LYNN UNGAR

MEDITATION ON ALL SOULS

Who are my people, where are you who birthed me
to play in summer's circle? I think I see you out of
the corner of my eye, gone before I can look again,
working, talking, engaged, and alive.

My ancestors are all about me in the ragged edges
of memory, like partially developed film; the details
are sketchy now. No princes and ladies among them,
but scullery maids and journeymen. I know their
faces, but not their voices, not the way their clothes
smell, not the soft hands warm and red from a day
of washing sheets. Did they smile at me? Did they
notice the little gifts I brought? I don't remember.

Bits of pieces of my people remain in memory's
attic, hardly enough to make a tribe. Forebears in
small brick cottages with sooty chimneys and out-
door toilets. Women with wrap-around aprons and
men with cloth caps. Brown teapots and doilies and
unheated bedrooms. My grandmother's slippers, my

mother's bone-handled hairbrush. Just memories, without the power to haunt.

So I seek a new tribe, other meanings. The little girl at the shelter shows me a toy, her creased fingers cannot yet turn a key, but there is still strength in her hand as it touches mine. Though she doesn't know my name, she would come with me if I would make her toy work and protect her from a world that has roughened her skin, bruised her heart, and given her only broken toys. She is a needy child; therefore, is she not my child?

The old man who hardly knows me says he loves me because I bring him a bowl of food and sit there while he eats it. He is a hungry old man; therefore, is he not my father?

At home I listen to a tape of sacred music and I weep in my chair, and I cannot say if I weep for the child in the shelter or for the child I used to be. The spirits have no power to haunt, I claim, so why do I weep in nostalgia and regret my forgetfulness?

I look at the faces around a meeting table, across the sanctuary, in the candlelight of a meditation group, and I think: these are my people now; we belong to each other; I pour out my soul in trust to a new tribe. These are my people, who touch my hands, who invite me to come along, who make room for me to sit in the shadow of the candlelight and listen to their songs.

ELIZABETH TARBOX

EASTER

The ducks came again this year. I like to think it is nature's way of making amends for the spring rain that floods our yard.

It is a gift for Easter.

When the fruit trees start to sneeze and the pile of snow thrown from impatient shovels melts down, the mallards come and make of our yard a sanctuary. They swim about and learn soon enough that this is a temporary pond, that it is too close to the highway for raising young, that there are energetic, impolite dogs in the neighborhood who see everything as a sporting event. The ducks know they cannot stay. But for a week or two they are there in the morning when we shuffle out with our bread offering; they swim with grace through the tall grass still showing above the water; they fly up suddenly and make our yard seem like a primordial lake from which the very birth of life has sprung.

And then they leave. Yesterday, I watched as the ducks made a turn about the diminishing pond, then took off with a whooshing of wings, freed from the clasp of gravity, and flew around above my head while I murmured: please stay a little while.

Easter is an exercise in letting go. It is a reminder that life is precious and fragile, beautiful and impermanent. It is a reminder that love is a gift of

immense proportions, that if we have shared it for
even so fleeting a moment as the time it takes for a
pair of mallards to sanctify our pond, or dawn to
come to a grieving woman who watches by a tomb,
then love has touched us and we will never be the
same again.

ELIZABETH TARBOX

CELEBRATE THE INTERVAL

Life is a brief interval between birth and death;
It is composed of a few notes between Prelude and
    Postlude;
It is a drama quickly played between the rising and
    falling of a curtain.

What shall we do with the interval of time?
What combination of notes shall we play?
What thespian mask shall we wear?

The transience of life tempers our joy;
Discordant notes reverberate in the soul;
The ending of the play is ever in doubt.

Yet the brevity can be rich with joy;
A simple tune caresses our ears;
The play produces laughter from time to time.

Why, then, are we so careless with time?
Why do we not sound the music of our hearts?
Why do we not feel the stage beneath our feet?

Is it not time to enjoy the interval?
Is it not time to play our own melody?
Is it not time for us to act our part?

Life is a brief interval between birth and death.
May we celebrate the interval with joy;
May we sing the song that belongs to us;
May we act as if our very life depended on it.

It does.

RICHARD S. GILBERT

REBIRTH

When the day is too bright, or the night too dark,
and your feelings are like an avalanche barreling
down the mountain of events outside your control,
when you look down and you are falling and you
cannot see the bottom, or when your pain has eaten
you and you are nothing but an empty hungry hole,
then there is an opportunity for giving.

Don't stay home and cover your head with a
pillow. Go outside and plant a tulip bulb in the

ground: that is an act of rebirth. Sprinkle bread-crumbs for the squirrels or sunflower seed for the birds: that is a claiming of life. And when you have done that, or if you cannot do that, go stare at a tree whose leaves are letting go for its very survival. Pick up a leaf, stare at it; it is life, it has something to teach you.

You are as precious as the birds or the tulips or the tree whose crenelated bark protects the insects who seek its shelter. You are an amazing, complex being, with poetry in your arteries, and charity lay-ered beneath your skin. You have before you a day full of opportunities for living and giving. Do not think you know all there is to know about yourself, for you have not given enough away yet to be able to claim self-knowledge. Do you have work to do today? Then do it as if your life were hanging in the balance, do it as fiercely as if it mattered, for it does. Do you think the world doesn't need you? Think again! You cleanse the world with your breathing, you beautify the world with your giving, you perfect the world with your thinking and acting and caring.

Don't stay home and suffocate on your sorrow: go outside and give yourself to the world's asking.

ELIZABETH TARBOX

PRAYER FOR THE HURRIED,
THE UNDISCIPLINED, AND
THE DISORGANIZED

O Spirit that hears prayer, attend to these words:
I would say a prayer for the hurried ones,
Those who are spiritually undisciplined,
Those whose lives are disorganized.

Thou must indeed hear the prayers of the deliberate
ones,
Those whose religious discipline is cause for
admiration,
Those whose lives are in good order.
Hear my plea for those who are in too much of a
hurry;
Help to slow them down to hear the patient word of
truth;
Attend my prayer for those who know not how to
pray
That they might still partake of sources of strength;
Let me plead for those whose lives are disheveled,
That they might know the sustaining strength of
order.
Help us understand that the still, small voice comes
to us,
Not only in the solemn setting of the sanctuary,
But in the hustle and bustle of our lives.

Help us know that sacred stillness sometimes greets
    us
When we seem least prepared to receive it;
Help us understand that the divine order of things
Supports us even in our confusion.
Let us seek to slow ourselves down;
Let us seek to cultivate disciplines of the spirit;
Let us seek to order our lives into works of beauty.

But, God of hurry and repose, Lord of discipline
    and impulse,
Spirit of the organized and disorganized,
Accept those of us who will never stop running;
Be patient with those of us who cannot discipline
    ourselves;
Bless us who never seem to get our lives together.

RICHARD S. GILBERT

NO PLACE TO STOP ON THE CROSS-BRONX EXPRESSWAY

I had driven through the toll gates at the George
Washington Bridge and was aiming for a lane that
promised transit through the Bronx. Cars whizzed
by me on the right and left as mine labored under
the strain of a 2,000 pound U-Haul trailer. The

gauge that registers the car's temperature was pushing toward the danger point so I had the heater blowing hot air on me to cool the engine.

At that point—with the cars whizzing by and mine swaying under the weight of the U-Haul and heat blowing at me and my atlas slipping to the floor and reopening on Utah—I thought I should stop by the side of the road to get composed, to cool off, to think things through.

But I looked for a pleasant, tree-shaded, uncluttered rest stop in vain. There was nothing, not even a shoulder where I could park and ponder. I realized, with a dart of panic, that there's no place to stop on the Cross-Bronx Expressway.

That image comes back to me when life goes faster than I would like. People whiz by me right and left. The weight of my befuddlement pulls me as effectively as the U-Haul on my car. I get overheated amidst sparks of energy emitted by those who surround me. I think it would be nice to withdraw to a neutral spot and contemplate.

But there is no neutral spot. Directions have been set, commitments have been made, processes have begun. It's like paying the toll on the George Washington—we're on it, we're in it.

I must say that I did just fine on the Cross-Bronx Expressway once I made it past the initial moments of fright. I rumbled along, switching lanes with

abandon as my trailer swayed, throwing an occasional Honda into a fright. I fancied myself a taxi driver,
fearless and free amidst the heat and grime.

And I was glad I hadn't stopped to cool off and
collect my thoughts. The hesitation would have only
prolonged the agony. It would have taken that much
longer to pick up the rhythm of life going on
around me.

If you watch my eyes, you may see an occasional
flicker of panic, but don't regard it with undue
seriousness. It's just the momentary hesitation I
sometimes feel before plunging into life.

After all, there's no place to stop once you're on
the Cross-Bronx Expressway.

BRUCE T. MARSHALL

MOVING DAY

The day I moved from the beach I took a last walk
along the spray-soaked pier.

The dawn came softly to Captain's Hill, and the
birds overlooked my tears.

I felt other losses, which ones I cannot say; just
memories, blunted now, no longer drawing blood,
but wrapped like phyllo dough around the place I
call my soul.

I need these times, though I'd just as soon avoid them. I need them to teach me things about myself I'd rather never know. These are the growing times, when I push myself to loosen the knots that tie me to old agonies and bad habits, to strengthen worn loyalties, and to find new paths to walk.

I took one last walk along the wooden pier. The tide was coming in. I'll not forget the way it looked that day.

ELIZABETH TARBOX

VOTING FOR YOURSELF

A friend told me of her entrance into electoral politics when she ran for office in elementary school. One thing she particularly recalled: It was a terrible breach of etiquette to vote for yourself.

That was true in my school too. Whether by show of hands or even by secret ballot, it was considered tacky to cast a vote for yourself. The neat kids would never do that.

This lesson was driven into me with such force that when I became aware of national elections, I wondered: Did the candidates actually vote for themselves? (My suspicion was that Democrats were too humane to do such a thing while Republicans probably voted for themselves—just early prejudice.)

In retrospect I wonder why that was such a taboo. If you go through the effort and risk of putting yourself up for office, surely you must think you're worth your own vote. Why was that so bad? One reason was the dread of being thought "stuck up." Another was our belief that if we really were good enough, people would know it. We didn't think we had to deal in self-promotion.

It was an innocent view of the world. But in growing up most of us learn that sometimes we've got to vote for ourselves. When no one else will stand up for us, then we've got to do it ourselves. When we have a belief that no one else is adequately articulating or defending, then we have to do that ourselves. When we are being hurt and no one seems eager to rescue us, then we have to take responsibility for ourselves. When it looks like no one else is voting for us, then at least we can count on our own vote.

My friend lost that big election in elementary school. She lost, you guessed it, by one vote. (The person she voted for won.)

Never let yourself lose by that one vote you didn't cast for yourself.

BRUCE T. MARSHALL

WORRYING ABOUT BOB'S WHEAT

One summer, we stayed three days at a farm in Pennsylvania where Bob and Minnie opened their home to tourists. Each morning we gathered for Minnie's home-cooked breakfast and talked about whatever we could think to say, such as the crops.

Bob was waiting for his wheat to be harvested. The crews were scheduled to come, then they postponed, then they didn't show up. The wheat was ready, the weather was sunny and perfect, but rain was forecast. "Maybe I should get somebody else," Bob worried at breakfast.

As we made our rounds of tourist stops, I found myself nagged by a vague concern. Nothing crucial but something that made me uneasy that I finally identified as Bob's wheat. I was hoping the crew would make it that day. I surveyed the sky anxiously for clouds. Though I would have welcomed a cooling rain, I was willing to put up with the heat for the sake of the harvest. When we returned to the farm and found the wheat still standing, I was disappointed. Another good day wasted—the nerve of that baling crew!

When I had packed the car before beginning this trip, Bob's wheat was nowhere among my concerns. It could have rotted, burned, been engulfed by grasshoppers—I wouldn't have known or cared. But now it became important.

I argued with myself about the appropriateness of this worry. If I'm going to fret, how about paying attention to something I have power over or something that makes more of a difference to me? I thought, how arbitrary: the things closest to us claim our attention and distract us from worrying about the right things.

But we don't have much choice over what claims our care (or, for that matter, our love). The issue is not whether we care about the "right" things, the issue is whether we care. My concern was not with the wheat, but about these people whose lives now were part of mine.

The day we left it hadn't yet rained. Bob waved good-bye from his tractor as we drove past his bounteous and uncut field.

I hope the baling crew finally got there. I hope there was time for Bob's wheat to be cut and baled before the rain. I hope he had a good year. I hope Bob and Minnie are happy.

BRUCE T. MARSHALL

WHAT IS HOLY?

WHAT IS HOLY?

We sat on the beach transfixed.
The moon not only glimmered across empty space,
But shimmered over a lake now calm
In anticipation of what was to be.

Slowly, timed by some celestial clock,
The curved shadow of earth moved across the lunar
    surface,
Left to right.
We could not see it move.
All we knew is that inevitably,
As if driven by some chariot-riding god,
It blotted the moon from our sight
Until the glimmering had become only a hinted
    circle of light,
And the shimmering was swallowed in dark water.

How long we sat there I do not know.
At last, tired in body and mind,
Refreshed in spirit, we silently left for sleep.

"Just another lunar eclipse," the paper said,
"Look again in December."
But there would never be another night like that.
Such moments are not repeated.
It was a holiness that will not fade.

RICHARD S. GILBERT

MORNING IN ZUNI

I had quite forgotten how to pray so far from home,
away from the sacristy of sea and shore, but then I
watched a boy chopping wood. He swung his axe
easily, slicing the piñon logs that were twisted and
bent like the hieroglyphs of an ancient language.

The slopes behind the boy were buttered with
sagebrush and sunrise, and his face was shining with
morning chores. And for a few precious moments, I
stood at his altar and caught the dimensions of his
cathedral.

ELIZABETH TARBOX

BOUNDARIES

The universe does not
revolve around you.
The stars and planets spinning
through the ballroom of space
dance with one another
quite outside of your small life.
You cannot hold gravity
or seasons; even air and water
inevitably evade your grasp.
Why not, then, let go?

You could move through time
like a shark through water,
neither restless nor ceasing,
absorbed in and absorbing
the native element.
Why pretend you can do otherwise?
The world comes in at every pore,
mixes in your blood before
breath releases you into
the world again. Did you think
the fragile boundary of your skin
could build a wall?

Listen. Every molecule is humming
its particular pitch.
Of course you are a symphony.
Whose tune do you think
the planets are singing
as they dance?

LYNN UNGAR

IN PRAISE OF DOUBT

It is not that we are not believers.
It is that our belief
Has to be passed through the fires of skepticism
And boiled in the crucible of doubt.

You have heard it said,
"Ours is not to reason why,
Ours is but to do and die."
But I say unto you,
Ours is not to doubt and die,
Ours is to seek the reason why.

When we doubt, we affirm the importance of reason
And our confidence in ourselves as centers of reli-
    gious authority.
When we doubt, we affirm the seriousness of the
    religious quest.
When we doubt, we recognize that truth was not
    engraved in stone 2,000 years ago.
When we doubt, we acknowledge that our under-
    standing of truth is imperfect.
When we doubt, we strengthen our faith.

For the faith of doubt we give thanks;
For the doubt of faith we make glad thanksgiving.
For the courage of adventure
That welcomes questions
As much as answers;
For the beloved community of seekers,
We sing our alleluias into the silent darkness.

RICHARD S. GILBERT

Grey, the color of the lake before sunrise; grey, the underside of the gull that flies overhead while the earth blindly searches for morning.

Give me grey. Grey the color of not sure, don't know yet. Grey the color of compromise, maybe, let me think about it; grey for talking things over, listening again, thinking some more. Grey for the shaded areas of the other point of view, for the possibility of change. Grey for the smudged edges of what once was dogma, and now is doubt. Grey.

In the bright red and green, and blue and gold of the season, and the noise and the festivity, give me grey, for the quiet of my soul, the moment of heaviness before sleep, the peace of meditation.

The steel grey of the lake mirrors the grey clouds overhead, and the bird meanders through the grace of morning flight, waiting, watching the movement of a grey walker watching him. The earth bows to find the dawn and feels its first slanting beams.

Can I take this as a promise, I wonder. That after the questions, the doubts, and the hours of contemplation, there will be gold through the grey, promise fulfilled and truth revealed. I don't know, but I believe in small epiphanies, a single beam of light in the darkness, some sought-for star, some one certainty emerging from the grey. Meanwhile, let us

embrace the doubt and cherish our unknowing and
patiently await the dawn.

ELIZABETH TARBOX

SALVATION

By what are you saved? And how?
Saved like a bit of string,
tucked away in a drawer?
Saved like a child rushed from
a burning building, already
singed and coughing smoke?
Or are you salvaged
like a car part—the one good door
when the rest is wrecked?

Do you believe me when I say
you are neither salvaged nor saved,
but salved, anointed by gentle hands
where you are most tender?
Haven't you seen
the way snow curls down
like a fresh sheet, how it
covers everything, makes everything
beautiful, without exception?

LYNN UNGAR

GOD IS A THREE-LETTER WORD

God is . . .
A three letter word,
Partner in profanity,
Companion of the sublime,
The deepest down darkness in me,
The rainbow wrapped around my shoulder,
The mystery beyond all knowing
or wanting to know,
The poet's literary friend,
The justifier of a thousand horrible deeds
and the why of a million-billion acts of love.
The question as inescapable
as it is unanswerable,
The macro-cosmic mystery
and the micro-cosmic explanation,
The word when there is a desert
with nothing to say,
And the subject of a jungle of books.
The without which nothing
and with which what?
God is the theist's joy,
The atheist's foil,
The agnostic's doubt.

God is a simple
   deep
     dark
       light
       bright
up-tight
   three letter word.

RICHARD S. GILBERT

AS THE CROW FLIES

A crow is said to fly in a straight line from point of
departure to destination, but that is not what I see.
Crows fly in sweeping circular arcs across the apron
of the sky, using all the available space from horizon
to horizon before settling on the top swaying branch
of the tallest tree.

You may think crows caw, that their voices are
harsh. But I tell you a crow can whisper to its mate
across a density of pines, and its voice is comfortable
and reassuring. A crow is mighty in its passion, vora-
cious in its appetite, and fearless in its flight. So I
aspire to live as the crow flies and stretch my soul to
meet the sky.

ELIZABETH TARBOX

SHOES

When Moses met God on the mountain
the first thing the Divine spoke of
was shoes. How are we to interpret this?
Where do you find God when
you have no mountain? Some say just
stand in the lowlands and call;
but you must be willing to take
whichever god might answer.

"Whoever would save his life
will lose it," said the prophet,
who was harsh, but never cold.
Once, driving across the steaming
lake, something beckoned, but I
was too impressed by the possible
to follow. Sometimes, in the
low light it haunts me. It will

share neither face nor direction.
It mutters through its hot breath
something that sounds like "shoes."
When I gave up high heels I heard
it fluttering around the window
for a month. Some nights I think
I will live into this obsession. Go
barefoot long before spring.

Some nights the voice blows in
from the Sound:
"Take off what binds you.
You are standing on holy ground."

LYNN UNGAR

SANGRE DE CRISTO

My names for god don't work here in the desert
because they are ocean words. I know how to stir the
mystery of the dark waters and move the spirit of
briny swells to life because it is my spirit, my mother
that rises from the waves to meet my call. And I am
not afraid.

But here I need a new language, a language that
loves clean white branches reaching to a blue sky
and the hard open mouth of a dry riverbed beneath
the canyon wall. Who are these gods that strike the
blood-red walls of the Sangre de Cristo Mountains,
where spruce and aspen with crooked fingers clutch
the wild wind's laugh?

I am ill at ease out here where ravens fly upside
down, huge feet curled with the ecstasy of high
flight, preening their feathers in casual command of
the wind's army. I can imagine being caught by a
hawk's beak, carried to 10,000 feet, and being indi-

gestible, dropped upon the desert floor. I can imagine thirst draining my veins, withering my skin till it flakes away. And I am less than I have ever been, because I do not know how to call the spirit of the mountain, or how to name the gods that move among these rocks.

Kindly, the universe puts its great lips to my ear and whispers, listen. Listen. You do not need to know the name of god, or call it. You need only to know that you do not know, and lift your face and stand in its presence and give thanks.

ELIZABETH TARBOX

ABOUT THE AUTHORS

Richard S. Gilbert is the minister at First Unitarian Church of Rochester, New York, and author of *The Prophetic Imperative: Social Gospel in Theory and Practice* and *How Much Do We Deserve? An Inquiry into Distributive Justice.*

Bruce T. Marshall is curator of the Museum of the Open Road. His books include *A Holy Curiosity: Stories of a Liberal Religious Faith* and *A Holy Curiosity: Exploring Religious Questions.*

Elizabeth Tarbox died in 1999. For two years before her death she served as the minister at First Parish in Cohasset, Massachusetts. Her work is printed here with the permission of her daughter, Sarah Tarbox. She is the author of another meditation manual, *Life Tides.*

Lynn Ungar is the minister at the Second Unitarian Church in Chicago, Illinois. Her work has also appeared in *Cries of the Spirit: An Anthology in Celebration of Women's Spirituality.*